T0196028

PRESS ON!

Awareness to Overcome All, While Healing Debts of the Heart, Mind, & Soul

CEECEE ROBINSON

BALBOA.PRESS

A DIVISION OF HAY HOUSE

Balboa Press books may be ordered through booksellers or by contacting:

Balboa Press
A Division of Hay House
1663 Liberty Drive
Bloomington, IN 47403
www.balboapress.com
844-682-1282

Interior Image Credit: Cee Cee Robinson

Print information available on the last page.

ISBN: 978-1-9822-5522-0 (sc)
ISBN: 978-1-9822-5524-4 (hc)
ISBN: 978-1-9822-5523-7 (e)

Library of Congress Control Number: 2020918050

Balboa Press rev. date: 11/05/2020

This message is dedicated to the Experiencer.

CONTENTS

ACKNOWLEDGMENTS

FIRST, I GIVE honor to my Lord and Savior, Jesus Christ. Without grace and mercy, there is void space. The English language does not hold merit to describe the amount of gratitude flowing around me. Thank You, God, for saving me when I did not have the strength to save myself, and continuous grace and mercy. Every decision follows a consequence, which intensifies as the unlearned time passes. I am humbled in having the opportunity to submit to Your will before my expiration of time.

To my parents, Clarence and Dolores Robinson. Yawl did that, and I love you so much! The strength that I have been blessed to witness in my lifetime is inspiration daily. Thank you from the bottom of my heart for everything! The sheer respect awarded to me since I can remember has not gone unnoticed. I see and understand the setup now, and both of you will forever sit as the functional threads of my heart. Rest in peace, Daddy.

Paige, I appreciate you. It feels amazing to have someone so deeply in my corner. Thank you for all your support through some of the hardest times of my life. *Oooweee! You already know …* This whole memoir writing experience is near and dear to my heart, and to share this creative process with you is a blessing. Your assistance is priceless, and thank you for loving me as I am!

Yoshina, thank you for your courage and support through this project, and life in general. Your son, Jai'Shin will always hold a special place deep in our hearts forever.

Denise, I knew early in the process that I had to use a photo of your smile. Thank you so much for allowing my vision to fruition. Now the world can see your healthy smile, it may even inspire smiles of their own.

Aquila and Umi, thank you for your time, support, and the motivation. It has truly been a blessing to experience cultural, intellectual, and spiritual experiences with your family, those same experiences contributed richly to my foundation today. Your authenticity is inspiration times two! Aquila, I would not trade our nerdy, creative, thirtysomething-year friendship for anything. I am grateful.

Ericca, thank you for encouraging me through my excuses, helping me type a few chapters when overwhelmed, and simply being you. I appreciate it!

Ms. Gertrude Green & Women of Wisdom, thank you. It has been a blessing to converse and learn from all of you bare handedly building the foundation of character in my life. I heard your testimonies of hardship from unspeakable circumstances, growing up with a lack of Civil and Women's rights. Through it all, each of you still rose high and taught me to see the strength within myself. God bless your souls, your wisdom will speak forever.

Writer's keep scribing your personal truths. Reading has accompanied me through…Thank You!

Family and friends near and far, you know who you are. Thank you very much for rocking with me Mr. & Mrs. Cooper & Family, Tara, Monique, Marci, Christy, Ms. Rita, Tracy, Fonece, Tiffanie, Sink, Ryan, Jackie, Deandrea, Dierdre, Deb & Mel, Pat, TC, and my late brother, Wayne. Many more names to mention, and I appreciate everyone holding me down in one way or another.

INTRODUCTION

HELLO. THIS MEMOIR is written through conflicting styles of emotion, by way of life's journey. It is recommended to read this testament in chronological order for best benefit and understanding. These events share validations of learning how to obtain the necessary strength to overcome fear and all its embedded sidekicks, which invoke inner struggles. Positive shifts in mindset are needed in the ascension of personal growth. Greatness is us; and humanity needs encouragement toward individualized deep thought. It takes a spiritual connection to safely search the heart for deeper truths.

This raw, soul-filled toolbox is filled with hearty doses of inspiration, insight, and motivation to the arts of healing all that exists. Life is not what it seems—it is infinite. Upon the understanding of this principle, the mental, physical, and emotional environments will illuminate personal truth. Being African American women, circumstances hold deep remnants of generational suffering, which are tainted by the debts of time. Life distractions can stand taller than Mt. Sinai, escorting pure and unfiltered shade that speaks only when spoken to. A shade hiding God's healing sun on purpose, enabling the mind to be anonymously robbed in the dark.

This world is busy, and without a healthy mentality, one's perception will fade to black as quickly as the speed of light. The darkness is tricky, yet no competition can stand against spectrums of light. But what if there is a cure resulting in the overcoming of the psychological experiences that sometimes accompany life's circumstances?

Empathy softly guides this complex journey toward all dreams deferred. Pain has been the best vacation destination to date—a vacation spot where the people around you disappear, and pain soothes to wakefulness at night. Beautiful, life-changing realities are born in destinations represented in this memoir. The epigraphs before each chapter represent live advice, quoted from the men and women who influence me through their profound writing proses. The poetry and other art forms expressed reflect real-time emotions traveling the peaks and troughs of my own spiritual journey. They reveal portions of hidden truth that could never be taken from possession.

Creativity is licensed and bonded by the spirit in the form of letters, each character holding unique dominance to the foundation known as the alphabet. Words manifest powerful magnets that create silhouettes of love, peace, and humility. Passion speaks with various tones that unite because we all have something in common.

This message comes from direct experience from many angles of uncovering emotional suppression of trauma. I touch on a few igniting my path of awakening, a state of control -less peace which allots time to perform checks and balances on spiritual debt. The processes of purging negativity offer variations of peace that are indescribable. The price of salvation is subjective and unique for all. However, when learning to grow through the debts of the heart, mind, and soul, there is no way in the world silence will continue to oppress. It is time to *Press On!*

Umi says shine light.
Society says do not.
What will you decide?

CHAPTER 1

Anti-woke

"I'm beginning to believe the killer illiteracy ought to rank near heart disease and cancer as one of the leading causes of death among Americans. What you don't know can indeed hurt you, and so those who can neither read nor write lead miserable lives, like Richard Wright's character, Bigger Thomas, born dead with no past or future." – Ishmael Reed

TURN OFF THE autopilot feature of human unconsciousness by simply pressing on! I know you are thinking, *Press what?* There is no physical button. The action of pressing is relative to decision. This process of personal growth filters the conflicting emotions of life built in an unaware mindset into becoming consciously aware of self and environment. Subsequently, this includes waking up to an active life free from the limits of fear!

Many navigate life blindly in a sleeping ignorance of bliss. There are generational gifts of pain left for inheritance, with no assigned beneficiary. The only requirement to receive is to not pass down a conscious mindset. In return, the recipient passes down urges to settle in an unawareness of mind, affecting the heart, which ultimately dims the light of the soul.

The laws of our land cannot be tampered with by humankind. Universal resistance is the only necessary resistance in life. If drama and negativity repeat, that is because the active cycle is doing just that: repeating. There is an effect paired with every cause. Resistance is key in maintaining elemental order. For an object to break, there must be additional tension applied. When problems exist, the effort it takes to run from these problems increase resistance in real time and often without notice.

Making a healthy choice to prevail through past emotional conflicts provides ease to tension in the present. Unhealthy practices of avoidance, suppression, and disassociation to problems alter the nature of duality, life's natural contrast. What would ebb be without flow? What is good if there is no bad? Could we go up if there is not a down? There is an opposite pull to everything to keep balance. Daily, there's significant urgency for the checkbook to balance, but does anyone consider with urgency the balance of the heart?

Negativity constricts positivity with attempts to overshadow perception, mirroring the heart's weaknesses. One's inferior projections feed insecurities from sources built up with unacknowledged inflictions of pain. Jealousy, envy, and pride are fragments of an inflamed mindset. Irritations in the psyche develop at the triggering of accompanying physical sensations. Most times after taking a pause in the present, we often realize the negative sensations are ill fitted for truth of the moment.

Why does the truth remain the story less told? Is it to shield consequences of deceit? Secrets can be a harmful way to resist. These covert messages can adversely affect the psyche, becoming a weapon of mass destruction, especially for the person who does not know. Some societal codes bond secrets with loyalty and trust. This can blur the line of virtue if secrecy leads to lack of self-worth and unhealthy manipulation.

An example of unshared knowledge comes to mind in reflection, after finding out for the first time I have additional siblings.

"Wait. Two more siblings?"

"Huh?"

"I am graduating high school, and they are years older with whole lives, and ain't nobody told me nothing!"

Come on now. Are these secrets necessary? An increase to resistances stalls personal growth. These actions can distort what a family can look like. The effects of secrecy and abandonment intermittently taze the nerves, altering a fragile shape of perception. However, remain vigilant to the possibility of happenings that cannot be easily understood or explained.

Be mindful of the circumstances that are being willed to others. Transparency fosters the approach to self-honesty. There is no fault. Only accountability can determine how unaware decisions affect others. A lifestyle of secrecy can cause an accumulation of heavy bags filled with emotion. Who wants to go through life holding heavy baggage in one's mind and heart?

The enemy is rapidly enticing souls of all ages and cultures away from authenticity. These villains take disguise in materialistic things, allowing something out of body in origin to obtain power to thoughts in order to possess psychological and financial control. A conscious change of mindset is the very thing that can stabilize these resistances. As conscious control lessens, the tension releases, catapulting a person into a mode of cognitive freedom.

Financial illiteracy plagues a pandemic of psychological and financial resistance. This oppressive tactic sets up positions of financial loss through what is not understood, and schemes. Do not get it twisted. There are many great lessons to learn in poverty. There is practice in overcoming setbacks of battling late fees, overdrafts, and eviction letters in perfect rotation. Instantly, this limited perspective of subconscious boundaries mirrors a false view of what can be achieved in life and who can achieve it. Experience is a great teacher, especially to the person who is aware of the need for learning.

Living from check to check is a continuous way of life. I witnessed my parents working hard but barely making ends meet. For me, working age could not come fast enough to contribute to keeping on the lights and water. Is it possible to instill financial literacy when this knowledge is not a makeup of reality? Ugh! Independence then measures by mastering the art of how to rob Peter to pay

Paul—the all-too-familiar consequences of living with "what it looks like" syndrome.

Conditioning of the mind is real! This country's many elephants outline a mansion of rooms, providing proof of violations against human and gender rights today. The self-proclaimed hierarchy of the majority teaches to look to an outside perspective for approval. An oppressed mindset deactivates the ability to embrace natural flow through life. Instant resistance happens when going against the grain of authenticity. Understand that there is a bigger universal picture. Everything is soulfully connected with intentions of greater good to align.

Civilizations of ancient history instilled morals of character into their people by way of tradition. If legacy dilutes with misguided power, anyone who disagree with majority could wear labels of warning or taboo. All with effort to detour one away from knowing who they are, and origins which they come. Be honest and ask, "Would I rather live a beautiful lie or grow beautifully through the truth?" Challenges did not start with you. They evolved through time, becoming a menace to all frames of mind.

Byproducts of hate leave humanity crippled with its contamination of influence. This disservice encourages people to dance outside themselves (without moving) to tunes of fear. This superstar power mutes the inner voice for selfish reasoning. These poisonous patterns generate a societal code that fuels many psychological afflictions now. Allow the universe to come to aid by dishing up the best life imaginable, uniquely customized, when one stop increasing resistance with the forces of their own way.

Intuition is a form of communication initiated by the limbic portion of the brain. This sixth sense of knowing has no explanation or proof. Spiritual communication is an attribute of this fascinating existence. I ignored my gut! Not my stomach but that deep-seated feeling of intuition, that knowledge of the difference between right and wrong, without logical evidence. Peculiar sightings, indescribable knowing, and spiritual gifts of discernment began early in childhood.

Even though my gut warned me about many issues, attempting to confirm these gut feelings with adults, resulted in the dilution of voice. Others fear watered, growing seeds of understanding with a gel-like substance, leaving the original concerns thirsting for truth.

Every second we breathe grants us the ability to make fresh choices. The nature of making healthy decisions widely affects the resistance. Consciousness is the vehicle that links attention to genuine intent. If the intent is pure, it could resolve inner and outer conflict to heal almost instantly, realigning priorities. This renewal will spring forth effective communication to bridge the gap of the inner and outer worlds. This is the transformation space where life slowly turns into living. Here are a few life hacks that will help to decrease the resistance.

1. Be present. Conscious decision-making is vital to life. Allowing the personality to dwell in the driver's seat of your mind causes harm to yourself and the people you love the most.
2. Slow down. Think before acting. Develop trust in the mind and heart to discern self-genuine intent. Trust your gut! No decision should ever call for the sacrifice of morals, ethics, and self-worth.
3. Become a verb. Switch actions' statuses regarding teaching, mentoring, and advocating to "in progress." Allow these verbs to become synonymous with nouns, becoming true companions to promote the fact that learning is infinite.
4. Let go. Dissolve emotional generational inheritances by not repeating the same mistakes that were committed within your family prior to you. We do not have the vision to see the future, so why try to maintain control every step of the way? Stubbing toes while walking in the dark hurts. Take the time to identify and isolate these areas in your life and observe where the most resistance is. And press on!

"Know thyself"[1], states its premise clearly and simply. These two words exclaim instructions deeply from the soul as a pun to magnify what is important. Popularity does not matter; even offering the key to the city cannot provide access to this distinct wisdom. Creation, God, Allah, and other synonyms used in acknowledging a higher power form the only key that will reduce and bring under subjection the conflicts in life.

Work is now in progress.

---

[1] Ancient Greek concept on the philosophy of self-knowledge.

Soul Canvas

Soft brushstrokes graze my abrasive memory.
Conditioned regions of the mind rebel
with hesitancy in releasing truth.
Allergic reactions appear on canvas as
Wet, dry, cracked, and smooth texture,
Splattered intentionally, with clairvoyance of resilience and wisdom.
"Ignorance is bliss"
Until
Awareness assaults and confronts preprogrammed thought,
Illustrating glimpses of soul's pure potentiality,
Uncovering illusions.
Hesitancy evaporates.
Colors energetically manifest,
Release beautifully.
Affliction is free.
The soul's art is priceless,
Unable to sell,
Even at the finest of galleries.

__Radio__

Counter resistance radio
tunes into self
to find *that* frequency
of *that* channel
of truth.

<u>Geometrics</u>

My life has changed drastically, yo!
Parallelograms of pain
Stained
From my elders' DNA.
Generations of mathematical errors,
X
Marked the spot for many,
Runnin' errands,
Breaking down boxes for Miss Prissy.

My life has changed drastically, B!
Obtuse emotions hyperextend.
Proceed with caution,
Willing to break ties of generational sin.
Victimized
By hazy eyes turned blind.

My life has changed drastically, son!
Hexagons crumble
When humanity's mother
Speaks!
Ground shivering in sync
With imminent paradigm shifting.
"Free verbs!" the people cry.
Few actions noticed,
Nouns resting, but why?

My life has changed drastically, homey!
A powerful rhombus of energy
Shines brightly through me,
Soothing spirits,
Geometrically shaping history.

Fundamentally relative
Of strength fought
Long, hard, and selfless,
Way before us.

My life has changed drastically, fam!
Mouths open wide,
Circles forming,
Experiencing God's love
Immeasurably.
Don't believe me?
Read: 1 Corinthians 2:9
In its entirety.

CHAPTER 2

Illusions of Time

> "Illusions commend themselves to us because they save us pain and allow us to enjoy pleasure instead. We must therefore accept it without complaint when they sometimes collide with a bit of reality against which they are dashed to pieces."- Sigmund Freud

THE UNCONSCIOUS PERSONALITY creates a rose-colored effect over one's vision, altering one's outlook of life and time. Doesn't that sound counterproductive? Many wander through life making assumptions, judgments, procrastinating, and ultimately making permanent decisions based on their projected realities. In self-defense, the mind automatically substitutes what is real with what is desired. Being caught up in pursuit of illusions strips away authentic power. The mental race begins when what is chasing does not physically exist. This negative defense allows the soul to perceive what it wants in order to protect the emotions of the moment from demise, initiating a false reality.

Tragedy is formed when this premise is used to encourage and teach toxicity to others. This disaster causes a paralyzing ripple within the atmosphere, fueling the greatest mediums of emotions regarding hate and bigotry to date. This creeper is elusive to sight. Some people think illusions exist only in magic. The paradox of magic is a brilliant breeding ground of the limiting factors contributing to unawareness. What's messed up is how easy it is to become psychologically distracted, causing a mix-and-match of time, action, and intent. This confusion prevents the ability to discern wants from needs.

<u>**Remember:**</u> Space and time do not exist in an illusion.

Unconscious reality gives the illusion of not having time. The devastation of realizing how much time is taken for granted brings a fresh level of alertness into life. Time is unknown and controlled by creation. The clock's innovation provides an instrument to quantify time. This measure is set as a standard for society to live on one accord. Spiritual vision within the third eye penetrates boundaries beyond the pressures of time.

Powerlessness is synonymous with fear. Unconscious behaviors and emotions are siblings: they may fight, but where you find one, the other will be near. These abrasions are deep into the roles of a fear-based mindset. It is woven into ego with a perfection. To alter the mind, one must observe current thoughts and processes, making positive, conscious adjustments, as necessary. If there are attributes of selfishness, there are usually feelings of resentment. Impatience carries sensations of alienation mixed with grief and anxiety. Make it a habit to oversee what thoughts initiate reality. What follows are some differences.

---

*"Look closely at the present you are constructing:
It should look like the future you are dreaming." –
Alice Walker*

Do not believe the hype!

There is call for the removal of blinders, barriers, and distractions in order to view reality from vantage point. Fear-based living leaves the door, window, garage, and screen door of the soul permanently unlocked. It leaves the automotive alarm sounds of *chirp-chirp* or *doot-doot-doot* as blankets of a false sense of security. This lifestyle leaves one exposed not only financially but also ill guarding the well-being of the heart and mind. A fragmented decision will only yield a fragmented result. To expect anything other than this derives from insanity.

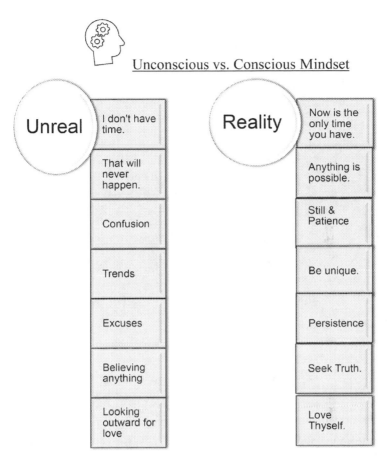

Unconscious vs. Conscious Mindset

Unreal		Reality	
I don't have time.		Now is the only time you have.	
That will never happen.		Anything is possible.	
Confusion		Still & Patience	
Trends		Be unique.	
Excuses		Persistence	
Believing anything		Seek Truth.	
Looking outward for love		Love Thyself.	

The alternate mindset of "lack thereof" will taunt the emotions of the mind to remember things you do not have. This detriment feeds illusions.

To experience love is to understand love.

The term *love* is one of the most used words in the English language. Its popularity in use highlights the intent toward its use. There are many aspects of this world which recall love, but do not reflect what love is. There is distortion somewhere. What are the experiences of love? In order to begin the understanding, there must first be love for oneself. The experiences and actions of authentic love acknowledge creation as whole. This experience does not resemble the following:

- violence
- mental/verbal
- physical/sexual abuse
- financial/emotional abuse
- deceit
- manipulation

These sensations are not sensations of love.

Love is unconditional, respectful, humble, and kind. Love is alive and encourages sensations of greatness! This energy has a light and vibration, allowing faster rotation at chakra centers. There are popular sayings describing this: "fly above," "transcend," and "positive vibes." These attributes arrive when consciously operating through creation, with no delusions in sight.

Programming is concrete. For business purposes, it is necessary to market in order to make money. There are algorithms in place behind the scenes to funnel the "right" content to the "right" demographic so the "right" people are distracted to constructions of reality. A show on television feeds on the psyche for at least an hour, and the mental investment may not warrant a return. Awareness is life, and if you are not aware, then, where are you?

The antidote to breaking the psychological chains of bondage is consciousness. Presence is the realm in of true reality. A conscience mindset attracts like frequency to like strengths. An unaware mind attracts like frequency to like weakness. Behaviors favor emotion: if one lives in the reality of pain and suffrage; then it is necessary to change the negative mindset to a positive.

When was the last time you visited La La Land?

Presence requires a keenness to self and to the space around you in real time. How often do you find yourself driving down the street submerged in thought, and suddenly arrive to your destination? These are times of non-presence. If there's consistent thought about past or future events in the now, this gives credence to mental chatter, leading to a thriving of the unconscious mind. It is okay to enjoy moments of nostalgia. These thoughts become destructive when the moment lingers, changing the mood in the now.

> "Everyday is a bank account, and time is our currency. No one is rich, no one is poor, we've got 24 hour each." -Christopher Rice

How are you choosing to spend your time?

Another illusionary mindset form leads to an unconscious spending of money. Money is a measurement of value. Time is an asset, and without it, there is nothing. Money will never have the power that time possesses. What happens once the material things are removed? Money cannot buy a new mind or soul. Choose to live illusion free by giving maintenance to self, as would the car outside. It is mentally embedded to care for things, yet societal support becomes dull when it comes to caring for self.

Create a positive medium in which to live. You are on a journey that will lead to abundance. Personal development requires letting go of preconceived notions and false realities the mind constructs from the circumstances of emotional pain. The soul is where the essence of being lives. Each of us has a unique form of nature. This level of awareness displays unity that mirrors life from foundations of good. Life's adjectives await in an illusion-free zone. Look at what is around; the view is beautifully clear.

<u>Time Is Money</u>

In my head,
A daydream of solitude finely shimmers.
Anticipating, outward nothingness,
Caused by lack.
Lack of nurturing the seconds
Flowing by faithfully.
As Father Krono organizes
His debits and credits
So that one day,
A bill may be generated,
Remitted for payment
Immediately upon receipt.

Illusion of Time

The illusion of time
Slowing down
Allows completion of every
Planned task.
The illusion of time
Speeding up,
Rushing
Into futuristic actions,
Mindlessly roaming
Into realities yet claimed.
The illusion of time
Going backward
Defies science daily
As you relive environmental pains,
Generational love
Misspelled, misunderstood,
And mis taught.
Evolving into a humongous source,
Feeding and festering
In multiplication with exponents
Incalculable.
Sickness of our people ...
Misaligned time zones capture
And hold hostage
Cerebral beings.
Subconsciously determined
With inherited strength,
Not to be captured.
Driving the will to
Travel inward,
Playing patty-cake

Through dimensions where
Time is absent.
Reality flipped inside-out.
The conditioning of time is
Confronted by consciousness.
Present wins!
Time bows gracefully
When consciousness observed
Through space
As one.
With no illusion left,
Time remains
Presently understood.

Primitive Math

Enough is enough.
Sliced erratically,
synonyms hesitate,
pronouns embrace
the circumference of trying
chance against fate.
Enough is enough,
said fast or slow.
International meaning,
yet transcribed by regions
misguided actions collect
It's dark season,
metaphorically speaking.
Enough is enough,
commonly mouthed
by the narcissistic
manipulating the script.
Is enough enough?
Chopped and screwed,
Rewinding accountability,
Exposing cerebral toxins,
Scientifically silly.
Naw,
You will recognize
Enough is enough,
If attention was paid.
Morals are sexy,
Must be fried, dyed, and laid—
An ergonomic slay!
It's okay.
"Enough is enough"
Is only a phrase.

CeeCee Robinson

It's simple math,
Context principles,
That saves.
No means no.
Apply,
Mean it today!
This choice is afforded freely to all.
Toxic behavior
Will fade
To lite-brite,
Naked potentials,
Bull riding positive change,
And *not* afraid.

<u>Humanity</u>

Citizen's arrest.
Refugees are arrested.
Who are Citizens?

CHAPTER 3

Mass Confusion

"There are three methods to gaining wisdom. The first is reflection, which is the highest. The second is limitation, which is easiest. The third is experience, which is the bitterest." -Confucius

DID YOU KNOW that fear and doubt were best friends? They are both emotionally centered within the ego. The personality takes shape by experiences of life. Egotistical behavior consists of emotional sensations that alter actions by the influences through perspectives of reality. If the ego's behaviors become tainted with doubt, then wouldn't it then be possible for visions to warp reality? We cannot replace the psyche, but the alteration of its level of control is necessary. If you take life and slide it in a shredder, look at the evidence. Are there manifestations of challenges reflected subconsciously from splintered spaces of doubt or fear? Iono.[2]

Acceptance of fear teaching is diversely sprinkled in every culture. These teachings are meant to discourage self-reflection and cripple an individual's thought process by default of the teacher's experience. As events take place in life, the emotional outcome becomes etched deep in the heart. Through un-acknowledgments of emotional pain built over time, these negative emotions harden and form fears in the heart. The emotional shards are the leading source for the development of judgment, opinions, and biases. However, it is common to forget the origin of painful memories of trauma, abuse, and neglect. This

---

[2] I do not know- in a southern dialect. Pronounced Eye-Ow-No

irrational system is in place by the ego and used as excuses to feed the personality. Folks sit back and ponder why America stands as the leading country in support of junk food. Iono.

Everyone has a right to an opinion. This is a beautiful truth. Remember, there must be mindfulness of the tainting that can happen when negative emotions silently influence opinions. We all know someone who falls into categories of limitations. A negative and out-of-control ego will lure thoughts into a state of confusion, catapulting thought leading from a false reality to second-guessing feelings of intuition. These foundations are clearly not healthy, so why does this trend continue to spread? Iono.

Personal fears and doubts are discussions that never came up at dinnertime. Shoot, doubt and I were in an intimate relationship. I worried about everything from what other people thought about my being overweight to how the bills were going to get paid. In hindsight, things seem to work out every time. My focus reduced to the things that could be seen by others, ignoring the self-seen, doing a disservice to myself.

In my daddy's voice: "You worried 'bout the wrong thang!"

Silence achieved grades of excellence in the wrong subjects. Being bullied dug a social trench, allowing outside influences to persuade and corrupt in full blown unawareness. Ignorance lead to sequences of unfortunate events academically and psychologically, out of fear of how intelligence look coming from impoverished environments. This lending of loyalty toward the wrong people leads to ultimately holding the wrong secrets.

Doubt lies in reserve with sexual promiscuity early on in life. These thoughts increase the immediacy to time and silence, resulting in an immature mind borrowing adult circumstances, allowing the subjection to cycle gonorrhea and chlamydia. Even though the diseases remained treatable, it could have easily been different. However, was the sterility of nature as a woman before starting a family worth it? Iono.

Examine the price tag of actions. This is not the time for shopping sprees and simply throw things in the bag. Fear-stricken risks attack the mind, body, and soul. Understand costs as a sacrifice instead of the price tag between the physical and emotional time lost, and infinite opportunities missed while living unaware. The sources of survival are encoded in the deoxyribonucleic acid molecule unique to us all. This soul depth strength lies dormant, waiting to connect from the inside.

Take note of the African American experience. Even though the world placed unexplainable weights of adversity on people of color, slaves consciously held on to cultural roots to teach offspring the way of the world, as best as could. Against all odds, survival is key. Just like the strengths of labor trickled down through generations, fear came with it. History shows there is no way around that. One can teach only what one knows. Just so happen, there is a wide gap on the disparities of a limited mind. So, when one understands, one must explain to another. The connection to self-places fear under subjection, allowing chronic frustrations to disappear right before one's eyes.

Operating from fear allows master manipulations of the mind. Remember, every cause will have an effect. Karmic balances calculate in real time with a timing deliverance of consequences to follow.

Guess what?

There is nothing new under the sun to be afraid of. Our Creator crafted each of us with the necessary tools needed to survive and compass these lands. Ancient wisdom teachings from tribes around the world instill principles and morals and encourage the journey to self. Is there a coincidence that these teachings have fallen ancient, and at whose expense? Iono.

Society is filled with shiny toys with instructions sold separately. The experience of overcoming obstacles in a healthy manner is how to play with fewer chances of an incident or emotional demise. The edges to life may feel smooth, sharp, prickly, or even blunt. These edges are accompanied by sidekicks of emotion presenting as anger, resentment, rage, hatred, jealousy, arrogance, self-pity, and greed. Behaviors and emotions are of direct influence on action, which then influence the karmic energy of a circumstance back to you in perfect timing.

Self-awareness has the power to defeat fear by shifting minds and hearts to recognizing the love and positivity within, infecting the household, improving relationships, forming great communities, and ultimately repairing humanity. Beautifully spirited cities are the new influence that attracts like-minded people and businesses in support of one another. People will begin to accept, acknowledge, and start healing as a nation, marketing in the campaign toward operation for the greater good of all.

Look around at the people who form your closest circle. Do they reflect the greater good, or do they enhance your least attractive character? Please take continuous inventory of whom you entertain in your surroundings; it will reveal a great deal about your own personality and strife. This may even be a great way to start documenting trends in realizing a baseline. Do not let fear make words like *failure*, *burden*, and *no* become a part of your reality. Within healthy realities, there are no such words.

My mother always tells me, "Nothing beats a failure but a try." Do not get it twisted; success is not equivalent to a win. If you try, you have already succeeded. Do not stop! It all starts and ends with you. If you tell yourself you cannot do something, you won't. If you believe that you can achieve anything, your passion-filled determination will overrule.

Stagnancy is for a pond. Cleanse the personality with universal winds by letting go of negative thoughts and behaviors alike. The conscious creation of healthy thought patterns will decrease and defeat the moments of fear manifested in life. I am learning that stepping into the unknown is where the affirmation "yes" is found. If it isn't, that is okay too. Try anyway.

Now that we have dropped off all those emotional bags where they belong, look in the mirror and fall in love again. Keep in mind that people will only tell you what they want you to know. Knowledge has no biases; research life. This intriguing thought becomes a seventh sense, lighting an undying fire of desire to seek the *why* for self. Iono is never justifiable to an existence of infinity.

An Emotional Dance

This mood swings
from left to right
rhythmically,
missing not one step!
On-time solutions
running late,
so I gotta compensate,
the steps
to accentuate the
mood.
Swinging
from dust till dawn.
Six o'clock comes quick,
a.m./p.m.
Or is it FM/AM?
All I know
is this mood keeps
swinging
from right to left,
missing not a step!
Energy expels
chemical compound solutions?
Failed!
That's all right, playa!
Green leaves sprout
From resourceful trees.
Knowledge
stabilizes
these moods from
erratically swinging.

Insomniac

Unknown origins of confusion
Travel slowly in the night,
Arriving to disappointment,
Carelessly handled in spite.

Friendship-like illusions
Wasting time of years passing.
Sudden onsets of judgments
Scream religious points of view.

Bipolar voices
Muffle God's communication,
Pathways tangled in webs
Of deceit.

Self
Knows that self
Cannot prosper for self,
Acknowledged now verbally.

But why can't I sleep?
Bobbin' and weavin', insult-filled gibber.
Only the size of a mustard seed,
Faith holds steady.

Confirming the known,
Synaptic clefts fire,
Intensifying sensations
To feel.

Hurt.
Disappointments.
This inflammation of trust
In the wilderness.

Antibiotics dissolve the "-itis"
At bay.
Bigger picture reveals slowly,
And I know
That now I can go to sleep.

Cerebral Hostage

Alone in a bushel of crabs,
Opposite directions attract despair.
Onlookers disappear
Once discovered.
Like minds don't always think alike.
Troubled in fear of tomorrow
While hiding from today
In the shadows of yesterday.
Wounds once healed,
Scabs peeled backward,
Leaving trails of serosanguineous doom
Through the marshes of clothing
Scattered, chopped, and chucked
At my feet.
In the darkness, a trumpet plays
"A Litany against Fear"
(A Christian Scott song)
With the valves of my heart.
C-flat
In a major chord.
Sound waves spiral silently
Into clouds of dust,
Hoarse,
Vocal-paralyzing agents
Dispersed mentally.
Since the beginning,
Doubt lingered in the daytime,
Usually around five o'clock
Traffic.
Allergies unknown.
No suicidal tendencies,
Tired of the mess
Smeared all over these walls!
As of now, this is the only place
I can call home.

Transparency

Grateful is as
Grateful does.
Concubine emotions
Escape captivity
Through means of
Awareness.
Onlookers gaze
In confusion and
In awe of
Wisdom.
Worn in bright colors
Of light,
Generated
Rapidly.
Twisting and turning,
Of the
Sacred place,
Deep in the
Wound
Of my spine.
Grateful is as
Grateful does.
Concubine emotions
Escape captivity
Through means of
Awareness.

I·will·overcome·it·all,·as·the·soul·cleanse,·through·the·
anointing·of·Creation.¶

(A·Litany·to·Self)¶

CHAPTER 4

Purposeful Vibes

"I am what time, circumstance, history, have made of me, certainly, but I am also, much more than that. So are we all." – James Baldwin

IT TAKES THE patience of spending time with yourself to acknowledge the resourceful energy flowing within. Light is unique in form and shines through everything. This illumination glows from deep. This spiritual connection is imperative to the fulfillment of purpose. The trials encountered through life create testimony. A richness in character develops from a library of consequences. The exposure brings clarity to passion. Aspirations are to be shared with the intent to help someone else acknowledge their purpose. Our souls' playdate is underway.

"I love to do this!"

Poetry is a second language that allows deeper connections with the soul. There is nothing like writing down emotion in a world full of metaphors and similes. In raw thought, the freedom of expression is ill![3] Casual conversation just won't do! I remember friends and acquaintances would recite and translate my poetic messages as broken or riddled. These criticisms sadly detoured from sharing things publicly, if at all. Through time and growth, shyness begin to fizzle away, along with caring how it looks to someone else, do not align with the soulful objective of life. The secret sanity of writing turned into cravings to document all life experiences.

---

[3] In this context, *ill* means "great"!

For instance, build a healthy working relationship with self to safely confide inward. Depending on the outside world alone can easily mislead. Experience an emotional release, with trust only the spirit can provide. Trust yourself. Physical weight can be heavy enough; it is possible to remain healthy by keeping the mind and heart free of self judgement and other emotional obstacles.

Dancing, singing, painting—are all soulful exercises. When I was growing up, music was a big part of the household, and it still is. I remember watching my parents sway and swing with their impromptu choreography. The floppy rug set the stage for expression, many times leading with me. The expression of the body's rhythm is positive emotion entitled to us all. Swing those arms, whine the waist, kick them feet ... Give yourself permission to move without judgment. Who cares what your body movements look like? Does it feel good? Simply enjoy yourself!

I spent beaucoup years adjusting my image of style for the satisfaction of others. Yet these same influences fell silent, when exploring deep interests of what truly made sense to me. Why? Because the physical representation could not remain physical. I had to act it and dress it, but it was not me! These purposeful activities will coast through spaces of letting go of the negative projections of self and everything surrounding. This public transit opened up a personal highway leading toward a properly filtered freedom with a one-way ticket to "Authenticity to be."

One mysterious beauty of life is the ability to feel. Everybody knows there's joy on one end of the emotional spectrum and pain on the other. Allow the self to operate from joy, in order to cope with the natural cycle of upcoming pain that will attempt to contort reality. This breathtaking destination is the place where life purpose is found. It is imperative to actively be you. This authenticity will equip you with a gloved hand to catch life's curveballs, no matter how fast, and release anything coming your way to distract your ambition.

One's purpose cannot be found highlighting someone else's reality. This is a solo journey. Consider the value in the time, and energy, spent toward investing outside of yourself. If there is no investment toward self, then there is a hemorrhage of resources flowing in the wrong direction. The unrecognized value has life changing resource available for growth. Unconscious mindset shed is major. It can feel like cutting soda from a diet or not eating fried foods, EVER! Light, clear, and amazing... When there is proper treatment of self, there is proper treatment of everything around you. Empowerment is an ongoing process humans must endure to extract the best qualities from life one step at a time. See what these steps may look like, in the following diagram.

Stairway 2 Better

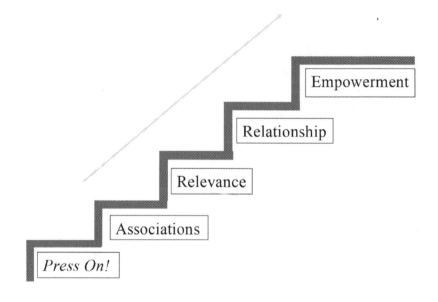

1. Am I aware?
2. Increase positive associations with everything around you. Release what does not fit. Toxicity does not belong within. Place unhealthy habits under subjection. Growth is enabled daily.

3. Understand there is a bigger picture and what your role is in it. Connect with self to define and refine beyond the matters at hand. Clarity leads the way.

4. Have clear intentions, building healthy relationships in your personal and business life. In order to do this, establish a loving relationship with self. Exercise patience in all things.

5. Self-empowerment warrants joy and peace. These feelings of success are only the beginning to infinite potential. Continue reaching, climbing, and pushing through all that awaits.

There may be friendships and possessions lost as the building of an intolerance to negative energy is in process. Please understand the things that disappear are no longer useful on the process to becoming better. Take action to move toward the goals that support empowerment in life. These clues are found in the conscious intent of the soulful activities, hobbies, and expressions that are genuinely enjoyed. There is no time like the present, and that thought is just as good as the seconds tick by.

The social butterfly nature lies at the abyss of me, yet socializing with people with bad intentions? Leads to a downside of living in mania, a forever hype entertaining false friendships. See, as passion thrives it rides to a voice of its own. This creates positive vibes that other people enjoy. Remain centered to protect it from energy vampires that may feed without consent. These instances define people who have all to gain in coping with their troubles but no energy to spare when the circumstances are in reverse. Unrealized or not, they end up being the only ones feeling better.

Unconscious play levels up tones of vulnerability. This opens dark hallways of manipulation to magnify weaknesses of the heart to see and be seen, marking as prey. Maintaining a high vibe is tiring, so why deplete energy trying? There is a distinct difference between optimism and high vibe. Optimism is an inclination to see the best possible outcome for any situation. High vibe is the action of enthusiasm with unspecific intent, also known as partying. Imagine having a smile or laugh twenty-four hours a day, seven days a week, versus effortlessly being.

"I can throw a mean party, though!"

Entertaining is an art form inherited from my father, Clarence. He was an exquisite chef, expressing levels of passion in stimulating the senses of guests through the overall vibe. It was not only with cross matching cultural cuisines, but also by setting everything just right. Everyone enjoyed his eclectic style and great attention to detail. My upbringing was Southern and old-school in tradition. Children did not mingle with adults at functions or in any other settings. That was okay because the sensations of my father's purposeful vibes did not stop at the walls. The healing warmth of love filled every room, to be in the house is blessing.

These are the sensations of comfort and assurance of things balancing to work out. What is hard is the denial of what's already uniquely instilled, further perpetuating struggle on the inside, and magnetically mirrored to outside. Purposeful vibes is about individual growth and defying the odds. To overcome adversity, we must strengthen the weaknesses of self, steady our households, tighten the community, and mirror these positive changes to the nation. Each one of us is crafted with precise purpose, and all of us are needed.

Life manifests in textures. An effective way to transcend change is to flow with it. Alter the desires to fit in and out of the body schematic of what "should be." Have a development of positive outlook toward self, resulting in an experience conducive to the joy of creativity.

You are what you think. You become what you feel. Defrost the smog smothering authenticity. The essence of a being is modeled and designed as a light source for navigating through the dark hallways of life. Shine it while taking witness to the phases destiny has in store for you.

<u>Simple Things</u>

I'm in love …
You meet me
Daily
Without prevail.
You soothe me
Organically.
Transference through time,
I *feel* you.
I gaze softly,
Mesmerized within the
Boundless.
Nocturnal-ish.
The day fades,
showing reflections of
The most
Beautiful,
Enchanting
Moon.

Basically ...

I'm basically basic.
Shiny toys
don't impress.
Fancy restaurants
leave me hungry.
Shopping sprees
are side effects of
manipulative programming.
I'm basically basic.
Club vibes
taint the music,
no comprende to
the language of signs,
falling on deaf ears.
I'm basically basic.
Yet fun leaks from my pores
naturally,
intoxicating the atmosphere
positively,
overriding
Egotistics.

Ear Hustling Destiny

Destiny speaks in a
Pain-induced labor of
Clarity.
Born in mass destruction
Through
Mass seduction,
Mrs. and Mrs. Ancestral
Formed,
Art of storytelling
Originating
From deep sea.
Atlantic-bound
Voice fluid with tears,
Leaking forward,
Now presents
The strength of overcoming!
Spirits ignite
In sparks of glee,
All credit being shipped and stored
Overseas!
Child please.
Yo lines of credit can't afford me!
My sun-enriched skin
and drenched kinky tweeds
Digress.
The code to freedom
Lies inside
Deeply.
Destiny speaks through a
Pain induced labor of
Clarity.
Born into mass destruction,

Purposely overwhelmed with
Mass seduction.
Sclera clear,
Sexy
When it's all three.

<u>Prose</u>

Swag is necessity
Confused with over-confidence
Ya know, ego fed lives.
Swag pushes the plow
Tossing up the alphabet
When verbal farming is allowed
Cultivating all senses
To feel the breeze
Dancing across the creases of the face.
Swag
Requires a mashup
Between thought and action.
Both provisions from ABBA
Through Grace & Mercy,
Soul filled feng shui.
Renewal penetrates deeply
Third eye,
Becoming our best asset.
Add heart
Finding greatest common denominator,
Of You.
Decreasing fragments
The ego left
In couplets of twenty-two's
Not on a Cadillac
Per say...
Swag is DNA
Fueling fearless hearts
While them Chevy's ridin' hot.
Rounding up fear
Stuck in survival mode.

Be who you want to be
Perceive. Execute. Achieve.
Swag
Remains perspective
Dissolving myths and lies
Historically fed inequities.
Distractions exist,
That lesson in school was skipped
To teach to think
Instead of run.
Purposeful actions lead
Tiptoeing
Through wisdom fields with daffodils,
And all other universal elements to offer.

CHAPTER 5

Patchwork

"Understand: you are one of a kind. Your character traits are a kind of chemical mix that will never be repeated in history. There are ideas unique to you, a specific rhythm, and perspective that are your strengths, not your weaknesses. You must not be afraid of your uniqueness and you must care less and less what people think of you." – Robert Greene

EVERYONE HAS CHARACTER. Character exists in different degrees to form unique personality profiles. Character lies at the center of thought, emotions, and behavior. The measuring of virtues is calculated by the action of intent on one's heart. Observe thoughts because they turn into attitudes. Attitudes pattern words, and words manifest into actions. Be aware of actions, as they can develop a system of habits into character. Paying attention to emotions is beyond relative; doing so refines the soul's strength to autocorrect lifestyles.

Patchwork is needed continuously in the building and strengthening of character. If fashion items become worn or abruptly filled with holes, the natural thing to do in preservation is to patch and sew it up. This thought has the same concept, but there is great emphasis on the conscious personality instead of material possessions. With a patched mind, heart, and soul, money will never have a place in the discussion. There is no differentiation between race, socioeconomic status, sexuality, disability, or religion.

Everyone should pause to assess one's active source of motivations in life. Introspection initiates a journey—not a thirty-day cruise to a distant land, but traveling toward the destination of the soul. This is the place of cleansing, healing, and raising energetic vibrations, enabling God's light to travel through and connect from the foundations of this earth. Unhealthy patterns in behavior smother life potential by highlighting character flaws over strengths. Limitations hide and fester internally through the emotional engravings of excuses. These soulful violations and injustices surface into reality in stealth mode. This highlighting of both positive and negative characteristics of the personality at the same time causes fray in the fabrics of life.

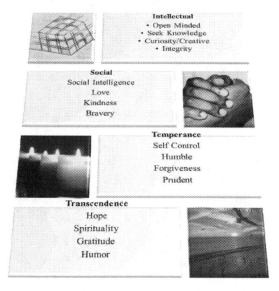

Photo Credit: Paige Cooper- Cube; Aquila
Lynch- Handshake, Candlelight

In the chart are classes' strengths. Inventory habits, emotions, and mindset for moral weaknesses. Then adjust actions with the strengthening of an underlying virtue to strengthen character, accessed subconsciously by the shape of what is known of our environment.

What Are Barriers to Patchwork?

- Negativity. It wins through the participation in drama, gossip, envy, jealousy, hate, and insecurities. These barriers arise from the fueling of life they are given from breaths spoken. Unfortunately, many mindsets are preset with cultural taboos and generational curses that promote the neglect to character strengthening needed to press on through social-emotional difficulties.

- Overcritical thinking, impulse control, and the inability to keep commitment. As soul strengthening commences, the inner world becomes actively alive and connected to the outside world, unveiling all the beauty surrounding you. This is critical to start the effortless paving of a new road in life toward your success.

- Low or high self-esteem. You are, until you realize you are not. A healthy attitude toward self should be neutral. Too much or too little self-esteem is character damaging, with each malnourished thought present with its own distaste in the presentation of you. It is crucial to reaffirm belief in self.

According to the law of magnetism, the energy of gratitude will attract more circumstances to appreciate in the future. If we express gratitude in every moment, we set ourselves on a course for things to appreciate in the future. With this law in the forefront of the mind and heart complete with understanding, grab a needle and thread, and let us get patching! The building of legacies is more than currency. It is about building the residual value of self for family and friends. It is priceless.

Did you know that being appreciative is one of the highest vibrations within your personal energy field? To increase the vibrations surrounding your life, simply be thankful. Did you know that you cannot experience joy or happiness without appreciation? It does not matter what your excitement is about; you are feeling thankful for something. These sensations bring involuntary smiles to all faces.

Underneath negative emotions lies a place of dissatisfaction. Are you a person who acknowledges what you already have? Or do you look at your life and immediately see lack? Attitude feeds both consciousness and energy. If you are someone who concentrates on what is missing from life, you are choosing to focus on problems instead of solutions. This way of thinking makes it nearly impossible to establish success now or later. Imagine filtering everything through deprivation. Examining the quality of expectations while viewing circumstances through scarcity will lead life to never-ending cycles of hot mess!

Every night before bed, try writing down the things you found appreciation for that day. There is no circumstance too big or small. Dissecting these emotions daily makes it easier to take note of subtle differences that occur. Moods are shaped by outside circumstances, but why? Things that happen on the outside does not have permission to alter personal reactions. If you are dissatisfied with what is found, exercise a power of choice to shift thoughts from the anxiety of the head to the strength in patchworking the heart.

There are all sizes of gifts in life. Do not limit yourself to thinking only about the outside world; navigate inside first. Acknowledge there is a process to building character. It is a birthright for the mind to function in a healthy and clear manner. Daily there are millions of decisions made affecting more than oneself. How many of those million points of view originate from healthy thoughts, feelings, and behaviors? Humanity deserves an optimistic approach. This place is between a rock and the starting line in a rat race of sanity. A healthy perspective will allow you to see there is no race that changes the starting circumstances in life.

> *"You wanna fly, you got to give up the shit that weighs you down."* – Toni Morrison

In society, there is exposure to many different things. People are often desensitized to life's value and their own self-worth. Is the concept of breathing too basic for acknowledgment? Release dissatisfaction while simultaneously embracing appreciation. Empower through the strengthening of current character flaws. Healing lives here. Unconditional love lives here. Peace lives here. Abundance lives here. These elevations of personal worth are just. It is wise to reevaluate and readjust old principles collecting dust in order to refine existence and understanding. No one is perfect. There is always room for improvement in all of us.

Alphabet Strut

May I have this dance?
Two-Steppin'
To similes and metaphors
Dispel.
B-town stompin',
Uniquely
Fearless and bold,
Dutty winin
With expectations
Or intent
To lyrically ascend
Through unfathomable dimensions.
But when you grabbed my thigh,
Our surroundings diminished
Down
To the dot of *i*.
Letters
Forming words,
Allowing us to
Be and come,
Literarily intertwined.

<u>Rah Rah Sis Boom Blah!</u>

I'll be a cheerleader,
Even when I don't care
For the team.
Flashes of smiles and laughter,
Rolls in stagnancy.
Mouth says one thing
With actions speaking differently.
Apples and oranges laced with
Tones of complacency.
Rolling tides of regret,
Left guessing how to play
The hands dealt.
Outside noises distract
Even a queen.
The king snaps back to reality,
Trying to find the you in me.
You either stay in or out.
The screened door remains closed,
Permanent choice evident.
The heart will know if it's authentic.
Gym bags of genuine love and desire
Dissipate,
Miraculously, into gases
Floating through the air.
Olfactory offenses
Flagged,
Leaving trails of
Soul ties strangled from despair.
A fate once known and cherished
Changes grown to take.
Morals crocheted deeply in my DNA.
So it's not in me to hate.

CeeCee Robinson

Be who you are,
Honey- just move out the way!
When you see me again?
I'll be on the other side,
Cheerleading silently,
Fearless and in full stride.

God's Plan

Extravagant thorns,
Extraordinary tears.
Triumphant blind spots revealed
Repeatedly.
Woke?
Then you know
To know
That you know nothing.
Schedules delayed.
"Hold on one moment,"
The operator repeats.
Silence.
Journeying on Route 44,
Lead by spirit prototype GPS.
The calculated route is filled
With detours
On purpose.
Trusting the invisible
Yet highly visible
Architect of all time.
Aligns stars,
Moon, and quasars
With soul light,
As faith in God's plan
Unfolds
Silently
In my life.

CHAPTER 6

Embedded Thorns

"In truth, pain is the price of freedom. And the moment you are willing to pay that price, you will no longer be afraid. The moment you are not afraid of the pain, you'll be able to face all of life's situations without fear." – Michael Singer

ALL HANDS ON deck! Passion is an understatement when it comes to nursing, especially being a registered nurse in the emergency, trauma, and burn departments. The intent behind performing a job becomes strength when the seams burst in the middle of the night with stress and chaos. This strength is needed in order to help people during the most vulnerable times of their lives—often death. Patients emotionally lean on nurses when they may not have a chance to lean on anyone else. It takes only minimal gestures to positively impact someone's life. The last thing a patient deserves is a disgruntled, bombed-out, lazy nurse! Customer service has always been a strong point of mine. I took the lives in my hands seriously without regard to acuity, race, gender, disability, or hospital politics, genuinely providing care with a holistic approach.

The work environment supports optimism in this craft of caring as encouraging through the long nights. The art of nursing simmers slowly from my soul. Working in the unpredictable trained me to be on my toes and stay ready. I adore advocating for patients. There is solace in knowing that these tailored skill sets could provide emergent care for anyone needing help. The synergy of night shift explodes as everyone works together, recognizing each other's strengths and weaknesses. God knew this unified character of work culture would show compassion and advocacy for me when needed most.

The birds coasting near the drowning sun goes ignored while in deep slumber from working the night before. *Boom, boom, boom!* goes the sound against the rattling bedroom window, kicking my heart into overdrive and away from REM sleep. A voice became audible, repeatedly yelling words about my brother, Wayne. In several seconds, the thoughts of a known blood clot in his leg after knee replacement rushed all senses, powering my body to involuntarily move with adrenaline.

An oversized gown and bare feet graced me out the door. In such a rush, my neighbor kindly closed the front door at some point; the confirmation sound of the door latching held no importance. Being close neighbors, my Mother and Brother gave easy access in times of emergencies. Their hallway appeared long with many doorways on both sides. A two-bedroom apartment would not account for the floor plan traveled to discover the emergency on this day.

The sight of him lifeless in a small space between the bed and the closet will forever be etched in my mind. Sure enough, his struggle was real. This entire event becomes blurry to memory and an embedded thorn in my heart. There was no room for panic. Wayne, my only brother, needed lifesaving skills in which I excel. Great technique and form provide effective heartbeats, but no matter the effort, God spoke to him, and he was called home.

What is seen can never be unseen.

The mental chatter of the ego chimed in, taunting me and trying to tear apart my career and emotions. Whom could I talk to about the effects of such a graphic nature on my psyche? Shoot, with a full week of insomnia, conversation became the new washing dishes. It is hard to express what is on the inside when the world on the outside just keeps going. Leaning on time's healing nature for thirty days offered only no work. All I could do was sit and watch the psychological thriller stuck on repeat in my mind. The voices somehow got a blanket and pillow and rested comfortably in my head, reminding me of not "saving" my brother. It says unpleasant things like, "You can't save anybody! You are a terrible nurse!"

It's one thing to hear something negative outside of you and learn to rise above it. It is completely different to process constant negativity streaming from your own mind. After a while, those thoughts manifested into reality. They encouraged fear of not being able to provide care for critical patients. It was crazy! It caused an anxiety before and during every shift as I consciously listened for critical calls on the phone and radio. I couldn't hide in the bathroom every time! The encouragement, positive thoughts, kindness, and compassion of the people around me was shown to me by people stepping in to take charge in critical cases as support during this process while I walked this infinite, winding path of releasing the wrongful guilt of performing unsuccessful life support to find something else.

Mere months passed full of reservations and anxieties. The frequency of feelings of doom were imminent on this day, so strong that I convinced myself that something horrific would happen to me, a car accident, while traveling to visit a friend fifty miles away. This feeling was different, with the urgency undeniable. Hands remained firmly on the steering wheel at positions three and nine, sitting straight up with eyes wide open, stereo powered down, senses heightened in order to brace for sudden impact. It brought extraordinary relief to exit and cruise through the various neighborhoods before arriving at my destination to find that she needed the aid of a lifetime.

I first noticed a well-groomed Pomeranian in the roadway, with a wide space opened at the front of the home. Immediately fight or flight emerged through awareness, allowing the feet to hover forward over the clean, smooth pavement. The car had to have parked itself, but it usually did not have those capabilities. When I entered the home, the intensity of oddness uncovered the truth. My friend's son, Jai'Shin, was lying unresponsive, and without hesitation or doubt, I administered the best CPR. He will always be the strongest toddler known. He was born fighting, strengthening like a warrior through his life shortly lived. God spoke his name that day to return home. Wayne and Jai'Shin influenced our lives and would live forever within our hearts.

Wayne S. Martin, a son, veteran, father, and big brother.
Brother, the consumption of your last breaths will bind us in a special way forever. God called you home with an exceptional job well done! Your strength to overcome inspires.
Alpha August 8, 1958—Omega February 17, 2014.

Jai'Shin Vinson, a son, grandson, nephew,
cousin, and so much more.
God's timing many times goes without understanding upon tragedy. I am honored to know Jai'Shin has a praying family with trust in God's will, above understanding.

Alpha July 31, 2013 — Omega June 29, 2014.

The reality, once glooming in thought, was now tangible. Things were so emotionally heavy: they could be picked up and placed in my pocket. So why not? Right? Save the emotion and deal with it later. A stronger time. Everything within my power had to be done to ignore the ego's tally of failures. The atmosphere was thick with humidity, and it was hot. Breathing brought insult to this hostile emotional environment. How do you choose to nurture the traumatic buildup of emotional wounds? The feelings of being worthless paid a toll from the heart, mind, and spirit, and I was out of change. Deep down, from an obstructed view, I knew that I did all I could. Not man, woman, nurse, doctor, or surgeon had the power to stop the inevitable of God.

Life has neutral energy. Reality takes form by the environments we shape. If there is unfairness to self, life will resemble this. If there is fairness to self, life will serve the same vibe in all circumstances. The mind is a powerful tool. Have you befriended yours yet? Only when there is a rapport established will the uncovering of emotional struggle appear closer than may seem in the heart. Life as it's known can change in a moment's notice, catching the unconscious mindset red-handed in distress.

Crash!

Heart racing, mouth wide open, and confusion set in while innocently accelerating from a red light. An unaware driver plows into the car from the left turn lane. The jolt confirmed the sight of entanglement and what my mind was thinking, what my ears heard, and what my body felt. As the burning pain deepened and radiated within my hips and lower back; immediately I thought, *What else?* Ladies and gentlemen, my first motor vehicle collision was born.

Switch! The roles quickly reverse to becoming a patient with not enough coverage, stalled interventions, and the inability to work.

Injuries began with a herniation to the lumbar spine, with nerve impingement. I also had excruciating buttocks pain, low back pain, burning sensations and weakness in my legs, a weak bladder, and limited mobility—and I couldn't make money!

Hold up! Wait a minute!

The complications of experiences currently are a challenge physically, psychologically, emotionally, socially, and financially. Wait right there; let me show you how God works! Just as you feel things cannot get any worse, it does.

A friend treated me to dinner out on the island for some fresh vibes. Great food, live music, and an open-air concept that fostered the breeze coming in from the Gulf of Mexico. It felt so good to be thought of and have a chance to mildly socialize after being stuck inside for a few months—soul feeding in progress. It was sheer coincidence a mutual friend was playing in the band. He spotted us and sat with us after his last set. We chatted so long that the restaurant was closing. He informed us a few band members were going to another spot and extended an invitation.

Upon arriving there, we noticed from the parking lot that it was a high-energy night. The jukebox line smeared into the crowd. The acoustics were good for conversation. Not even fifteen minutes later, the others joined in, but with slurred speech and extreme energy. As an RN, the erratic behavior these gentlemen were displaying symbolized an impairment of some kind. This lowlight placed a damper on the mood, and with unanimous decision, it was time to go home.

When Keeping It Real Goes Wrong

This man became aggressive with whomever he thought had his car keys. After witnessing him shove target one to the asphalt parking lot, I removed the keys from her hand like a relay so that he would leave her alone. Too slow! He saw it and charged. My first instinct told me to run, but my back and hips would not let me. It did no good to try anyway because before I knew anything, he had hold of my clothes, ripping them from my body. In terror, the keys blindly flew. This experience felt like we were playing an involuntary game of street tackle football—but at midnight and on major highway. I am thankful for the traffic patterns that night; this could have ended tragically.

This entity looked me straight into my eyes while squeezing both of my hands as hard as he could until there was an audible *snap*! The pain, the struggle, the fear, and the unknown of what was to happen ran across my mind, all while standing numb in the dark. Out of nowhere, another man appeared between us to stabilize the violent drama after onset of injury. This tango with the darkness uncovered shadows of fear that hadn't been acknowledged in many years. Being helpless under the stresses of violence and pain felt strangely familiar. He had a grip on me physically, but the reveal of a bigger picture was commencing emotionally and spiritually. The only clear thought remaining was the oversized ashy red door in the corner of my mind. What the heck?

Nobody ever told me that pain would do me like this! Life becomes confusing upon experiencing physical, mental, emotional pain every day, all day. Sanity begins to shake while thoughts cloud with darkness, dimming the soul's light. This illusion filled crevice invited feelings that remain too unsavory to list. Pain is the primary vessel God uses to restore and renew. Pain is an object of emotion. It is often taught to allow these circumstances to go unacknowledged, leading to the collection of excess weight and baggage. Enabling darkness manifests a reality full of hurt and disappointment through life. Pain will most likely happen, but the question is, how will it be endured?

Chronic Pain

Burdens
Victimized
Through a lover's eye,
Killing the love
From her.
Dying cells of grief
Clump slowly,
Pseudo cascading
Out of control.
Flips, twirls, flops
Of life,
Filtered through
Insanity,
Distorting gravity,
Recharging cells
Anonymously
Into believing.
Slippery slopes of illusions
Provide instabilities,
Causing emotions
To tumble
On high heat.
Burn injuries
Gain soulful
Respect.
Rekindling fire
Of love
Through the pain,
God ordained.
Uncomfortable,
Life analysis brings
Remembrance
Of creation,
Including the rocks,
And I remain
Highly grateful.

What Is Normal?

What is normal?
A standard of the masses?
Numb and tingly,
Weakness in legs riddled
Neurologically.
What is normal?
The spasms in my neck?
Normalcy can skip me!
Muted voices
Muffled with
Lullabies
Ringing irritatingly in tune.
Am I product
Of imagination gone sour?
Trends and fads
Remind a rewind-type lifestyle.
But I wanna fast-forward toward understanding.
Destiny sculpts
A magnificent peace.
So, "normal" must be me!

<u>02/02/2016</u>

Today is the day that changed my life.
Vehicle collision out of nowhere—
Bang!
Here comes strife.
Aches and pains
Flow down the drain,
Recycling daily.
Lawyer who? They can't help me
If they have no degree in alchemy.
The dotted line remains
Synonymous with money.
Broke as a joke told on Doomsday.
Never would I have thought of
Meeting myself like this,
Face-to-face.
Missed understandings exacerbated
Times ten.
I look to my left, then my right,
And cannot seem to find my "friends."
Illusions drift while
The game of hide and seek never get old.
All it takes is for you to go through;
Spiritual sight shows the difference
Between glitter and gold.
Thirty years of running fast
Through time and space,
Giving all my lunch tickets away.
Left hungry and unable to feed my crown.
Today is the day that changed my life.
Disaster
Catapulted me into his veins of grace.
Slowing down,

Healing the perspective of eye.
Preparing for an alternate route
That only the Spirit can drive.
My tears are still present,
Although they exist through faith,
Painfully broken
With salvaged goods that remain.
I am somebody,
Even if I don't have a dime!
My wealth lies in Spirit,
And my best friend is time.
Keep pushing through
What seems to be unfair.
This may be your very protection
From despair.
Today is the day that changed my life.
This journey has been the hardest yet.
Even death wouldn't suffice.
Salvation does not come easy,
And I ain't seen nothin' yet.
Fearless!
I sit or stand,
May even walk with a limp.
But my flesh no longer binds me.
My spirit of discernment
Has been pimped.
Testimonials of freedom
Unite the lights.
I ain't goin' through all this for nothing.
Soon, I will jump back in.
Everything happens for a reason.
I dare not question Thee,
I'm just humbly thankful I am free.

CHAPTER 7

The Red Door

"You may not control all the events that happen to you, but you can decide not to be reduced by them." – Maya Angelou

IT WAS TUCKED away deep in a real-life creepy way. This door was dusty and cobweb covered, with vintage fixtures—the total elephant of the room. The rest of the things lying around in my mind were frilly with dulled color. These fragments of pain went unacknowledged until what appeared to be in slow motion, *Snap! went* the bones in my right hand (at least the cast was a glittery purple). The dark entity revealed pushing me headfirst into the opening of this "red door." Have you ever been forced to do something feared? Boy, looka here, the poison behind life's struggles need to be discovered.

Which decision is appropriate for an eight-year-old? Street racing competing with other children from the neighborhood while riding bikes? Or the indecisive task of choosing which Saturday morning cartoon to watch? Both, duh! Unfortunately, it is the latter, exploring outside of home should be adventurous, or so she thought. No one at any age, after leaving their safe haven, should be bombarded with repeatedly peeling away dry, ashy, musty-smelling fingers from a trusted older teen who thrives on erasing the innocence of a child. This is not just any child, but me.

Daylight stir the butterflies chasing each other in the pit of my belly. It leaves me squeamish, but I cannot articulate why this feeling persist. It is bad enough that I constantly feel like something is stuck in between my legs, even when nothing was. The sacred essence of my childhood experienced repeated internal bruises and scratches. Too much to understand or deal with, as a child, I could only do the best I knew.

It always felt like there was a bright sexy neon hologram hovering above that only preying eyes could see. Pedophiles seek prey carefully. They automatically sensed who can be taken advantage of with less risk of anyone finding out. This craziness is stuck on repeat. Maybe it is the new normal? It will simply take some getting used to. There were many texturally coded lessons throughout these intermittent yet surprisingly continuous runs of sexual deviance. The perpetrator changed, but the acts were always the same. Does that make me good at this?

Due to stage in adolescence at time of sexual exposure, immaturity completely blocked understanding. The clues that can be found on the outside of what is happening are embarrassing. Due to improper care of a seemingly early menses, caused soiling of clothing every time. This otherwise alarming sign is not telling of abuse because shortly after my vaginal trauma began, so did it. These encounters began to shape the beginning of an unhealthy perspective on sex and menstruation. Sores of abuse left a twisted way of processing the word *no*, altering future deviances with ease. Does no really mean no? If so, then why didn't they stop when it was yelled repeatedly? The consensus prove otherwise, society can sometimes feel so backwards.

There are boxes everywhere!

Sexual deviance debos[4] the innocence of men and women daily. Many abused voices are confiscated and confined to a box, which is hidden deep on a shelf at the local sheriff's office and labeled "cold." It is time to repurpose the box of innocence. These premature actions cause a major misguidance to emotions, self-worth, distortion of reality, and the psychological pain of being tossed like a rag doll. At

---

[4] Takes.

least there were no physical beatings, so it was safety presented with a twist—or so I thought.

It is dark and hot in here, and these knocks are hard!

The venomous secrets scattered around aid in unconscious promotion of "falling victim to." When there is a misunderstanding of this concept, it jeopardizes every aspect of life, from communication to morals. "Falling victim to" is not hot in these streets, ever! This truly means that something is off and there is dire need to press on in becoming aware in order to restructure and reroute away from the unhealthy. Abuse travels across borders of age, race, socioeconomic status, and even religion. Think how easy it would be to "fall victim to" when there is no awareness of being a victim.

So that is where the construction of this door began?

Fear ate me up on a new level and has been nibbling at my soul ever since. The city felt inside out this night. The lack of cars on the road, the darkness, and isolation from the flowing winds ushering hazards. Once I noticed the inside door handles of the car were broken, I knew he needed no directions to take me home. The involuntary captivity status change deeply opened vulnerabilities that have never been before faced. Running is no longer an option. The personality along side of me is covertly filled with the ability to deliver sinister acts of violence, and I ain't even know it. Those initial feelings were empty compared to the volume of terror awaiting destiny.

But why?

Forcefully moving from room to room through this haunted house bore new sadistic adventures. In one, we sat on the floor for hours with a butcher knife pointing inward toward the left side of the throat. Other injuries bled and began to swell, but the swordlike knife, ironically, never pierce the skin of my neck. It did not matter how hard or long he held it there! My instincts told me not to move, and that was just what I did! There is something about being placed in a situation to wonder, "Is this the way I am going to die?" while every hair on the body salutes the present at attention.

The different chambers in this home felt ready to welcome me as guest. The troubled host preached his self-righteousness beliefs all night until he did not. Something about women that act soft need to grow a backbone…? Iono, because all along, a different conversation was in place between mind, body, and soul. Angels were encouraging, reassuring, and nurturing behind the scenes of a spiritual reality.

Valid thoughts of no one knowing where, who, what, or why this was happening gave him a pass to act out twisted fantasies, using me as his muse. The outward cries began to turn coldly inward, accompanied with steady streams of tears. His boredom to my obvious courage trigger an increase intensity. The ability to endure sheer vandalism to the body with pride, excited thoughts of his psychological thriller games of silent torture that sickly continued for years in the background. Abruptly, as if he were running late, he physically let me go. Ladies and Gentlemen, his new sick game is called freedom.

No authorities were ever notified because of the multiple wagers on my life. And after witnessing his public humiliations of madness, it felt true. He did this so well, I involuntarily blocked every real-time emotion associated with that night. Till this day, I'm not sure where those emotions went. It was enough for me to have my life and the opportunity to heal the physical receipts left from his madness, burying the emotions deep. Until now …

What did I do to deserve this?

Something must change! The spirit of promiscuity, only lead down paths of destruction and even death. I escaped death, but there are many people who do not get that chance. Here I am, fortysomething, and I am just now making a conscious decision to heal these past pains. There is no telling how long this red door could have been hidden in the mind. It is never too late. Excuses are real;

they appear out of nowhere as allies. They are something like a shield of protection but are used in defense of the perspective of pain. I knew them all too well. This disease looms on a road frequently traveled yet less discussed. Abusers master the art of inflicting pain through pain, and the abused master how to become a beautiful, mirrored reflection of just that, pain.

Clichés of ignorance varies through culture and play a role toward complacency in the silence of violence within the community. Words are powerful weapons. They are sourced to code communications of destruction. The trick is to manipulate away from learning, further encouraging contentment for what is told and unfortunately providing a feeding frenzy for weaknesses of all kind.

Have you ever heard, "You are a product of your environment"? Well, no you are not! You are the product, and the environment is the environment. Familiarity of a thing does not validate it as one's truth. It never will. If one looks like something, that does not mean it is something. This evolution of negativity can and will play tricks on the mind, heart, and soul. In a manipulated mindset, it is easy to fall victim to it all, especially when the root cause issue has attached in the abyss of the soul. Talk about manifesting illusions of anything! Search there; infinite solutions of healing await.

I am scared.

An irreconcilable pain was accessed with the fracture of my hand. The anger, frustration, disrespect, and violence led me to this mental void of stench. It is disgusting to find these weeping wounds left unattended for decades this deep in my mind and heart. As the assaulter battled his demons, there was a confrontation with my own. The packages that once haunted are now pierced with light from the opening of the door. The dust will settle while I break down these boxes and begin to painfully heal.

Silence

Silence is golden, almost to a fault.
They rubbed, touched, and yanked,
And through silence, I fought.
Silence is golden, almost to a fault.
As the naysayers' manipulation
Shield silence from thought.
Silence is golden, almost to a fault.
Stillness provokes higher
Thoughts.
Sliced and diced,
Thrown in a melting pot of forgiveness.
Silence is golden
Now an alchemist is born.
Enlightened.
Wisdom granted, yet almost to a fault.

<u>Journey</u>

A fragmented journey on an unfamiliar path.
Intertwined,
lethal combos tango,
assaulting humanity's intelligence.

Climbing mountaintops, conquering life spiritually,
mastering the art of seeking truth.

"Joy comes in the morning," wisdom silently alerts.
Strife does not last forever.
Sure, it hurts.

There is no reason to frighten and cry.
Popularity is a humanmade contest,
It is designed for the loser's passion to die.

Continue to choose the light.
No longer willing to sacrifice sight
with solving a fifty-thousand-piece
puzzle at night.

Attempts of fear fight won't stop
Fragments divinely debug,
Cleansing spirit, as we float fearlessly to the top.

Stillness speaks

through volumes of lust,

bursting the seems

of my journal.

CHAPTER 8

Stillness

"I don't think many people appreciate silence or realize that it is as close to music as you can get." – Toni Morrison

STILLNESS IS THE absence of movement or sound. Its synonyms soothe the English language with tranquility, peace, and calmness. These nutrients of life often go masked by the erratic control of the unconscious mindset. The last thing the ego wants to lose is its voice. Ask yourself, "Why would the ego quiet itself in order for life to speak to my emotions from the soul?" That would be too much like right. Many times, people ignore the synonyms of stillness until calamity contorts life as it is known.

This is a life-changing state with experience varying from person to person. The often difficult process justifiably allows the credits and debits of life to balance. A spiritual connection is an antidote for the miserable effects of toxic consequences that cause backlashes and inflict psychological, emotional, physical, and financial harm. The time in stillness is *never* to be taken for granted. There is great potential in this time for permanent growth.

The chaos-infused challenges in life are worth confronting regarding their origin. "Why are you here?" Untwisted, conscious mindsets are aware that infinite wealth is received when one understands the value of life. Obtaining spiritual wealth will flow with the application of effort. This juggle is performed through expanded awareness, as the soul strengthens simultaneously. Unpleasant circumstances become light enough to resolve or change the position of mental importance to focus on what is important. This four-concept juggle revolves an experience of living in wholeness.

- 25 percent communicate from the soul
- 25 percent recall the principles of God from Spirit
- 25 percent transcribe understanding through the actions of mind and heart
- 25 percent adjust delivery with relevancy and tone to present
  = One Hundred percent effort applied

You will never know how to do one hundred percent of it all. Know that learning takes forever because knowledge is infinite.

This process does not represent any old time period of life. There usually is a tragedy or unforeseen event that seemingly throws life off balance. The reliance on sayings of hindsight lures us backward into a false sense of security to think post mistake effort is okay. It takes having a proactive and preventative thought process activated simultaneously in mirroring healthy methods to cope. It is easy to get caught in moments of nostalgia from unhealthy perspectives. This ruins the momentum of effort achieved while juggling to distract present contentment with past anger.

Sit with me in life's incubator of stillness as together we shine light on the realities of coping. Feelings of helplessness, loneliness, and uselessness are a part of a seductive evil. The diagnosis of depression and posttraumatic stress syndrome are recognized in stillness. I sit at home, alone with intrusive thoughts, shaky mood, financial dependency, and arthritic pains in every joint of my body. At the lowest point of life, these evil projections look and feel hella real, and will trick the mind into believing suicide[5] is the answer. It is not, get help! It is the connection to God that saved my life. Manmade things, other people, could no longer help me.

During timeless reflections, memories fade into sitting around groups of smiling people waiting for the inevitable turn up. Nine times out of ten, this turn up's common denominator had me all over it. Until the reality of being alone abruptly stops the "friendship" boats from sailing through streams of fakeness anymore, exposing truths to plain sight. Thinking reveals things about people that were mysterious to once blind eyes. The sensations of loneliness began taking over thoughts, actions, and vibe. This medium became perfect for depression to thrive to its all-time best.

Loneliness is an antonym of stillness. The feeling holds negative connotations with the inability to cope with being alone. There are millions of people emotionally crippled by this daily. This condition is taught by sight more than financial literacy. Remember, the children are watching; you are not invisible. These emotional images can be seen in more than literal sight. The body's miraculous functions act as detectives assisting to figure things out. It is up to us to listen. While growing up, I always heard, "The truth is hard to handle." Is that why there are so many lies? What happens on your street happens globally. How long will life remain idle but in drive? Dealing is acknowledging. Forgiveness is dealing with the intent to press on.

---

5 National Suicide Prevention Lifeline 1-800-273-8255. Open 24/7

The active force of stillness is here. The depths that pain travels can only be revealed one layer at a time to grasp the truth surrounding existence in the simplest form. The mental and emotional substitutions of truth's reality are left exposed with nowhere to hide. This highlight of lies, manipulation, abuse, and assaults used to hurt me with the power I gave them from hurting myself. This pill should have a choking hazard on it. By far, it has been the hardest pill to swallow to date.

"Punctuality is a respect for time, tidiness is a respect for order, and positive thought is respect for the mind." —Peter J. Daniels

---

Deep down in my womb, intuitiveness tells me this seemingly demolition process has purpose. Slowly yet surely, everything known collapses in a puddle of unfamiliar fragments. A psychological break is inevitable because a process of remolding has been ordained by God to reorganize my pieces. Crying is magical. This purposeful cleanse waters seeds of action with reverence and spiritual strength to overcome. It becomes medicinal with the understanding that all things are working together for greater. The decision to release control to a higher power was the first conscious decision of my life.

There is a thin line between peace and insanity. This process is full emotion. One minute there is understanding, and then as healing begins, new doubts surface as deeper afflictions become challenged. One challenge was a general anger toward men. This sensation attached itself to a short fuse of dynamite. My mood became a blanket of severe agitation used on a cold winter day, with *any* disposition from men. The men that I knew had my back are all deceased, it was the living men that seem to find ways to hurt me. My psychotherapist prescribed involuntary time to unwind at a psychiatric inpatient hospital. The medical team became concerned of homicidal ideation if provoked. Convincing these people otherwise was impossible. How did she sense such deep emotion, was it that strong?

The definition of *humble* became understood in this facility. The loud, constantly shifting, volatile environment is terrifying to say the least. I remember thinking how in the world am I supposed to get better here? There's exposure to various degree of psychological disorders, in complete crisis mode. Talk about an eye-opener!

After releasing the shame of being here, it became therapeutic to exercise the scientist in me to observe others who were vulnerable and unstable in their own crises. I have experience taking care of psychiatric patients, usually there's limited contact with the patient being housed behind a locked door. But it is another situation when you are behind that locked door, and the tall bob wire fence stops you from walking forward. If access to outside is even granted at all. While staring at the gate, from the inside dayroom, I trade the crayons for a half pencil.

Dayroom Shenanigans

(Written poem translation) When alone in the dayroom, all I can do is stare at the gate. If offered the chance, I will escape. There is no privacy, all is exposed, and the chemical romance is void. My ears don't deceive me, the yelling, displeases me, and paranoia is trapped in minds that need healing. This taste of insanity is yuck! Naw, for real, nasty as fuck! Osmosis is real. Somebody, anybody, please come and get me!

Coloring helped to reconcile the unattended emotion swirling sporadically consuming my heart. Some of the other patients made it a habit to watch, slowly I had a little crew join me. The nurses were shocked, but thankful to see the active engagement with something productive. The conversations at six a.m. over the unlimited basic coffee, were filled with delusions and paranoia setting many tones for the day. We patiently awaited our fate as the psychiatrist called us one by one into the office to reveal the day's plan. Maybe it is God's timing to be here, and maybe here to even help someone else?

You know, it is until realizing everything one "knows" to try while coping with the conditions of life fail miserably. Reconciling the amount of emotional turmoil from decades of suppression, dumbing self-down, discrimination, manipulation, sexual abuse, coupled along with disproportion of sacrifices from bad decision making makes one try the inevitable from the place of desperation. Finally, taking the wisdom heard all my life to lean into God, and like never. After sprawling out in the floor, in prone position for unknown time that day, my ego died, and I been looking up ever since.

In order to press on, there has to be a choice to endure and flow with whatever comes. Clarity hugged me tight and encouraged an open mind to this experience, after all I had no choice. This further enhanced my perception of goals toward becoming unbound by pain. Hurt people hurt people, and this vicious cycle will end. Silence becomes a new power instead of being a symptom of fear. This four-day experience capsized the years leading and will alter the years that pass. When it was my turn to hear "you can go home" from the psychiatrist, I shared that portions of this experience would become documentation in my book. Ironically, to their belief, my verbalizations were perceived as grandiose…

Lucid Dreams

Words fall from the shelf
At night in form of
Puzzles.
Mismatched alphabet,
Too many *U*s and *I*s,
Languages decipher,
Hieroglyphics style.
Ancient waves of knowledge
Intercede the mundane,
Awakening an essence
Of being.
Martial arts,
Subliminal fight
Winning!
Awards of freedoms
Merge the *U*s into *I*s, that B.

<u>Passion Speaks in Form Of ...</u>

It could have all been different.
Sacrificed
To the street of streets.
Tangled up
With nowhere to run, hide, or sleep.
"All streets lead to jail or death"
Filters through my head.
Fighting embedded scripture,
Floating deep beyond life's threads.
Total eclipse of the sun,
At my worse,
I lie and cry,
Wishing to hear sweet lullabies
Of what sounds good.
Paying souls train fare,
Blinded and unaware.
"There's a war going on inside of you!"
A voice calmly yells.
"Give in and let me salvage your broken pieces."
My heart translates well.
And ever since that day
The silent conversation was held,
My ego died,
Leaving myself
To become less of self.

Still is Relevant

Life experiences guide
down foreseen path,
decisions made.
Altering
east from west,
merging north into south.
Mysteriously,
the middle becomes
perimeter around the heart.
Pages turn
constantly
with no end.
Growing into
You.

CHAPTER 9

Inspiration

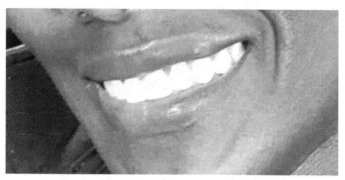

Inspiration lives in a smile.

THIS PHENOMENALLY DIVINE experience is the birthplace of an idea. Ladies and gentlemen, I call this … inspiration! Inspiration is defined as having mental stimulus or feeling something of creativity or enthusiasm. Ah-ha! If you are reading this book, it means that you are alive and breathing. The process of breathing has inspiration and exhalation phases. On inspiration, oxygen is inhaled through the nose, and at exhalation, the byproduct of air is blown out through the mouth. We could apply this same vital concept to the process of meditation. One must first acknowledge and observe breathing in present time. Once this happens, infinite opportunities open in the mind, leading you through yourself and to a path specifically for you in life.

Do not dismiss ideas that come to you in the middle of the night during insomnia, or the thoughts that come to you while you are juggling multiple tasks. Allow the positive ideas to flow in bypassing the ego. Shut down the appetite to have the attention and control.

Scribble the ideas that come to you in the notes section in the back of this book in silence. Once ideas are spoken, the game of offense becomes intense, and the distractions create "just something else" to do, with that something leading away from the great idea. Motivation allows for positive feedback aiding to clear unsavory circumstances that presents. However, inspiration is the sum after adding action to thought. Please note the press on math solution below. This can be used to factor life to find hidden sources of inspiration.

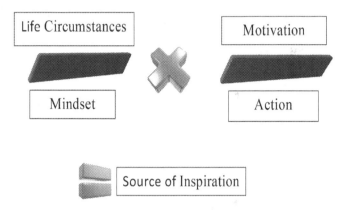

For example: Take an active mindset which mirror life's circumstances, and factor out all negative influences, and negative belief systems. Use the clear canvas of what's left, to express motivation through natural fearless actions. In this healthy place, sources of inspiration will meet you daily.

Behind every action lies a motive. This motive is the why of the action. Thoughts are powerful and manifest into reality. It is necessary to consciously shift thoughts to the *why* end of the spectrum instead of *why not*. Many times, people subconsciously cruise on autopilot during a task, prematurely giving ongoing distractions to the pearls of clarity in the moment. Be attentive to the reasoning of action and make sure it remains consciously clear of selfishly desired outcomes. Why make moves that cause robotic anything? Press on! All you can do is what you can do with what you already have.

Who Are You?

Opening to the motivating wonders around is a guide to self-realization. This process is inevitable for the living. It is unsettling to hear people say, "I'm not the creative type." The complex process of thought creates avenues for creative sparks. There are infinite ways to express modes of inspiration. Not only does inspiration tie you to the present moment but it promotes a universal connection with the world around you. This world needs your steadfast passion for its very preservation. There is no passion too big or small; every atom balances the same.

Rewrite Your Story!

Everything is not always peachy, and no one is perfect. There are going to be times that attempt to darken the hopes of everything! Lurking shadows create a disguise to obstacles in life. Please do not become rigid at this time. Learn to dance not only in the rain but also with the shadow. Personality flaws must be acknowledged to initiate healing and transform weaknesses into strengths.

You can do anything imaginable in life. There is no script, only a journey. No two journeys is the same. Dwelling within the present will help ward off negativity and fear. This perspective stands as protection while traveling through what is unknown. Your GPS and other technical devices cannot navigate through to the soul. In the moment of inspiration and motivation, one can harness the gift of spiritual guidance toward the road less traveled.

Society's collective cannot quantify against your one.

Success is nothing more than a subjective and emotional trophy. Success is *pressing on!* The sensations of success activate when there is action to follow the first choice of the mind and heart. Trying something new, or a remix of the traditional toil, means going down roads with buildings of innovation. Do not be afraid! Your swagger is infinite. Your ideas are worthy and needed for fueling the community. Seeds of discord and suffrage have run amok within the psyche for a long time. Uncover the free ability to shine light into the darkness of life to expose the crippling thoughts of *can't, won't,* and *no.*

Do not predicate motivation with money. There is a global trend right now to secure the bag. Making money is great! Many dream to financially support their families and their own desires. However, making money should not be the primary focus. When the focus stays on the craft or message, the money will come in perfect timing. Money is a form of currency that holds a neutral energy. This allows money to take on the energy of whomever possesses it. Take note of your energy surrounding monetary things. Once the real purpose of money digests in entirety, there will never be a lack of it.

You will remain aware and make healthy choices to continue just actions with confidence. Look back for what? Retrospect? Currently, the past is only good for points of reference. It has indeed passed. The now is where flowers bloom, and inspiration will allow your blossoming into what you are: infinite possibilities. Be willing to invest in yourself. Everything you need is inside of you, and integrity is the trophy to gain.

You are unbound by the trials and tribulations of life.

Your consciousness supersedes what is tangible. Stand up with courage in the healthy choices you have made thus far in a new perspective. As the funk legends Parliament-Funkadelic exclaim with high energy, "Flashlight!" These surges of high energy felt from music inspire the body to move rhythmically to the beat. This medicinal effect can be experienced from writing, dancing, painting, rapping, poetry, or singing. This not only encourages creative expression; it nourishes a medium of support during spiritual awakening. You are creatively alive! The megahertz rains six sensory explosions, and some 808s[6] will have your life on fleek!

Inspiration fills the buckets of fear and doubt with hope and faith. Wisdom comes from numbering your days right. There is a humbling experience that happens when one can recognize limitations and focus as though everyday matters. There is no circumstance that will negate these premises. Remember, you are armed with a flashlight of authenticity. This light illuminates' action versus what's simply spoken. You are boundless. Never detour from sharing the gift of you in the present. Somebody somewhere needs motivation through inspirations of overcoming.

Evolution is needed for growth. Growth and changes happen on a micro level, which causes a shift of mindset from fear to "I can!" At some point, faith in a higher power must initiate to accurately trust the process when there is no logical explanation. The unknown is where destiny lives. The creative window of opportunity is open and waiting. The time has come to ride a new kind of momentum that is authentically designed with empowerment on the inspirational path of being you.

---

[6] Nickname for electronic drums used in hip-hop music

Auditory Erections

She plays that saxophone
Like she knows what I need!
Encouraging moods of love
In the daytime.
Loud, proud, and free.

My ears become erect with anticipation.
I wait.
With intent to know
The origin of time
This sound traveled from.

Organic in nature,
Rooted.
With divine seating
Reserved.

Senses heightened through realms,
Communicating with the inverse of self
In parallel dimensions,
Where saxophones
Play the human as an instrument.

Cries of freedom
With every breath.
My ears remain erect because,
This is beautiful.

Through It All

Hurt
Brain,
Hurt
Thoughts.

Achy frame
Jump starts
Before the clock starts.

Pow!
Racing to finish.
(Get back, Jack!)
I'm feeling
(So much)
I'm contagious,
Straight chicken pox!

This itch manifests
Will to scratch
Dreams deferred nine times!

Settling in the heart's muscle.
Four chambers of love,
Unconditional spasms
Feeding loins
Deep.

Time stands still
Next to me,
Whispering
In my ear.

Senses connected
With sights of strength and prosperity.
Standing between you and me
In its inadvertent appearance
Of air, space, and opportunity.
Through possibilities
Infinity.

True observation exists
Through flaws,
Discomforts of pain,
Healing
In God's grace.

The Light

Texturally awakened
Through broken pieces of glass,
Complex
Cortex fearlessly shattered.

In due time,
Pineal glands spark and shatter!
Making realities easier to see.
The shadows and light tango
To a funk beat!

The softness in the effort
To smile
Taken for granted.
Firing firm, thickened skin
Now covered with rashes.

Textures awaken
Patiently.
No ifs, ands, or buts mumbled.
Tears say it all
In a secret coded language only
God hears.

Believing!
Magnetize soul pieces,
Bonded with paradoxical glue,
Ignored by plenty over the few.

Stop, drop, and pray!
(The heart yells.)
Acknowledge and surrender to God

Allows notice of
The sun's spell.

Flirting where nature dwells.
Following all days,
An anonymous number.
No time to flaunt,
Be nurtured with a universal understanding.

Presence
Debunks the illusion,
Causing societies mishandling,
Psychological madness,
And confusion!

Stand awakened!
It'll be all right!
Uniquely alert,
Shining light.
Brokenness equals a billion-piece puzzle,
Is where He works best.
Trust Source,
Joining alignment with the Earth.
Living nothing short
Of God's will.

CHAPTER 10

Cracking the Code to Freedom

"Don't come into the presence of God to impress Him with something He gave you." – T.D. Jakes

FREEDOM IS ACHIEVED by first acknowledging bondage. Bondage antagonizes freedom in physical, emotional, and psychological forms. The effects of mental bondage place restrictions on the understanding of being free. This misfortune automatically reshuffles the psyche's priority lists in limited insight. One may even suggest that Prison is the only source of bondage. This is widely off balance to reality. Bondage with a dose of limited insight, unknowingly, compound missed opportunities that are presented daily to confront them. It is critical to release damaging thoughts and develop inner strength to overcome the mound of an adversary's hauntings.

Conscious decision-making is vital. One must become open-minded to voluntarily seek one's truth. Consciously exercise the power of free will in everything. At the end of the day, dealing with anything other than reality is a choice to neglect the self. In return, stacking the odds and emotional weights of bondage with yet another height of affliction. The time in the eternal clock is ticking away consistently and without judgment. Tomorrow is not promised.

This world and everything in it is God's gift to us. Believe in a cause that sits higher than the self. True freedom allows the breeze of the universal elements to cleanse cycles of misery that have plagued intentions for centuries. A freedom mindset costs nothing, yet taken for granted, the price can increase drastically. It takes a living acknowledgment of God to transform the daily mundane inactions to conscious living. It is often the circumstances of our flesh that enhance negativity and strife. True freedom possesses the real power behind the feelings of success, productivity, compassion, happiness, joy, and tranquility. These attributes can become hyperactive in life when one submits to the grace and mercy of God.

Positive Attitude, Loyalty, and Kindness Is Being

Sheer existence, while displaying humility toward everything, is the reset space to allow the soul to become an active participant toward cracking the code to freedom. Abundance lives. Breathing has divine support that anoints opportunity for all to exist. Go shopping internally to fill these spiritual carts with the nutrients needed to tell friend from foe, truth from lie, and good from evil. Journey inside yourself; you do not need gas or money. Free will is needed to focus constant attention on the intention. Allow this process without fear's big head in the way. Begin by shifting the unhealthy thought patterns that support demise. Refresh by training the spiritual filter to catch and release all things harmful. Realign priorities to reflect the healthiest of spaces and enjoy watching the peace that precedes.

The study halls of life's pitfalls and virtues reveal understanding of how the game of life is played. It is possible, to only play with the cards or circumstances that are dealt. The primary focus is needed on the game as a whole which include dreams, goals, and what can be done to transcend what appears to be a spades games with a hand full of hearts and no spades. But it is in the day-to-day practice in the affirmative that alchemy is born. This mind, body, and soul effort prompts further research into self to strengthen one's generalized moral weaknesses.

It is mandatory to remix the mindset to refurbish the behaviors that are in play. Affirmations are great tools to display this. How we look and speak to ourselves are key components to sort. Speaking in the affirmative not only raises energetic frequency but also places the ego in check. Write, read, and repeat. The brain is a muscle and remembers the thoughts that frequently travel. Guide the thoughts with sentences of self-worth reflecting on the improved vision. Let us look below to practice speaking with affirmations. In full acknowledgment of God being in control, proceed with I am...

You Are Worth It!

Push beyond limits with use of vision. There is profound difference between vision and looking. Looking leaves vulnerabilities to only see what grasps at your mind's attention. Vision is a sense that allows you to see, and filter what you see through awareness simultaneous to discussion. In this state, the harness is open to all that exists. If you stop and think about it, there are people who would give up everything to have vision. Do not take a view, especially an unobstructed one, for granted.

Clean Up Thoughts by Forgiving and Letting Go

Freedom allows things that were once barriers in life to release and then transform into reference points on the evolving path of growth. Problems fade, worries lessen, and everything becomes more easily done and understood. Healthy decision-making happens consciously and with ease. Dishonesty becomes intolerable to do or to deal with from anyone. Clarity heightens the flight above structures of complacency. In those bright skies, it is clear enough to see that being a victim is an occurrence encountered, having nothing to do with one's identity.

The Matters of the Heart Speak Volumes to Life

The present offers protection to cope. Staying aware overrides the past's unaware emotions to view circumstances from a third-person point of view rather than the intimacy of first person. This psychological spacing secures the clarity of the Now against toxic sensations that may be stored in the heart. As practice increases, enlightenment fills space. Keep in mind, manifesting spiritual healing is the code to freedom. This process is the common denominator for living your best life. If it was easy, then everybody would be doing it. Do not be afraid of working on self, your emotional state depends on you to reconcile its mishaps through time.

Affirm:
Today is a Great Day! I am humbly grateful for the perspective of continuous learning, adapting and living in a state of purpose and peace. As I overcome these layers of pain, I understand great lessons come from it. God is the source of light. I am a conscious soul, reveling in Today, acknowledging God's promise of this moment.

Revoke Access to Negative Thoughts Now!

"Press on!" is the subliminal switch located deep within consciousness to operate from the position of mindfulness. This spiritual level is where creation communicates. Awaken the psychological slumber of pain, insecurities, and other debilitating characteristics of negativity. The mean thoughts that terrorize do not have permission to have control today. We possess the authentic right to live in prosperity. It is essential to soulfully establish life to an "open your harness" approach for infinite potential. Engulf your mind in using tools of creativity or sources that allow alchemy to turn negative emotions into positive experiences. This is harmless to the body yet therapeutic to your heart, without the active judgment of the mind.

Freedom reflects the mental space mirroring the view of objects within reality. Life's unlimited texture can spread crust smoothly enough to fill illusions, obstructing one's view of the itemizations soulfully tallying against. Cracking the code to freedom is about identifying what forms the crust in the first place and evolve from there, gaining spiritual and emotional intelligence along the way. To Understand what we go through has direct relevancy to the consequences of the accumulation of soul debt. The mindset holds *the* key to shift itself to realign with an active universal consciousness. Acknowledgement is vital to overcome it all-while healing the debts of the soul, unlocking psychological emotional chains of bondage.

The payment of attention is now due. This subconscious spring cleaning allows for a cocreation experience to annihilate negative habits and behaviors by strengthening character to sow fertile seeds of integrity in life. Do not get it twisted; the pandemic of darkness has an antidote, and it is light. Salvation has a cost, and daily life picks up the tab. All things are now possible, so live! In Detective Alonzo Harris voice, "Do you want to go to jail or go home?"[7] Both can easily become reality. Even though the destination may present differently, the actual choice remains the same.

---

[7] Quoted from the movie Training Day, a character played by Denzel Washington.

Nature's Exhibition

The rain claps against earth's crusty shell,
stealthily sliding the periphery
congregating to center,
delivering moist messages of Truth.

Disrespect,
humbles in growling winds
disintegrating malformed virtues
to an atom, molecular in weight.

Unconscious thought swells the air.
Duck-in & Weavin' the moon,
lightening demands clarity through,
erratic tag-teams with thunder's muscle.

On command,
the atmosphere chant rituals,
in a pre-ancient language,
praises of unity.

Naked & Fearless,
Mother Nature moves in silence.
Nurturing all species to cleanse,
on exhibition while taking a shower.

Lunar Moments

The moon reminds me
Of you and me
Intertwined,
Surely
destined for ecstasy.
The moon reminds me
Of emotion
Felt,
Horizontal and vertically.
The moon reminds me
Of translucency.
Vibin' to various
Realms of truth,
Slighted by more than a few.
Healing wombs emerge
And flow.
The moon reminds me
Darkness is penetrated
By beams of light.
Awareness leaks while
Eroticism awakens.
Organized confusion
As the moon shifts,
Consciousness waves erratically,
Motioning for your attention!

<u>Connect</u>

Electric currents flow
Engulfing life,
The birds,
The bees.

Pollinating
Buds of kush
Seducing variations
Of truth.

Power
Disconnects with
Ill calculated moves
Lost in shade,

No were to go,
Everywhere the same.
Blame,
Even turns lame!

Eclectic sensations
Don't come out,
Travel inside
Dodgin' pride,
Finding what sparks.

Divine connections
Mind, Body, and Soul,
Balanced
In flow.

Consciousness births understanding
Common denominator
Factored in tools
Of Fibonacci.

Translucent to sight,
Canals trickle,
Persistent peace.

Parallel with time
Intertwined through space
Connected to God's grace.

An Experience of Awakening

The anonymous
Funnels fear-laced
Hormones
Straight into the dome,
Products
Carefree.

Truth hurt,
Pain is temporary.
Perform due diligence to self to see!
Overgrowth trimmed,
Signage still sitting in the street.

This time on the right.
Vandalized and swaying,
Words awaiting the clear
Of pathways,
Intentions,
Clarity
To be.

From the stars
To oceans,
To Pluto and Mars,
Complexities
Go undefined.

It doesn't matter who's thinking,
U or I.
Human minds won't see.
Do not look to man

To explain
Everything,

Take actions to
Heal the soul to whole.
With acknowledgment of Spirit,
Oneness will unfold.

Peace and joy
Vibrate at an exceptional rate,
Making the heart flutter, skip, and jump,
Obeying fate.

Keeping faith
Continuously,
Transforming life's adversary
Into a priceless abundance
Of God's rarest pleasantries.

Press On!

XOXO Thank You!

NOTES

ABOUT THE AUTHOR

CEE CEE'S INSIGHTS toward problem-solving are gifts from divinity. Her compassion and advocacy of personal growth, aided by shifting thought to motivate humility, are unprecedented. Empath abilities drive the principle of understanding faith in God and strengthen with the fruit of her continuous labor to speak. She loves listening to all genres of music, laughing, seeking knowledge, and motivational speaking. She currently resides on the Gulf Coast of Florida with her loving partner and two fur-baby felines, Pancakes and Big Boi.

Please visit ceeceerobinson.com for access to her podcast, "The Vibe Clinic." She administers weekly doses of positivity, and other mixed-media expressions of wellness and spirituality.

Email questions, comments, and inquiries to:
Ceeceerobinson111@gmail.com.

Printed in the United States
By Bookmasters